fresh

NOTES ON

CUSTOMER SERVICE

TREAT THE EMPLOYEE AS #1 AND
THE CUSTOMER AS #2 AND YOU WILL
GET CUSTOMERS FOR LIFE

MICHAEL D. BROWN

GREENLEAF
BOOK GROUP PRESS

Published by Greenleaf Book Group Press
Austin, Texas
www.gbgpress.com

Distributed by Greenleaf Book Group

For ordering information or special discounts for bulk purchases, please contact Greenleaf Book Group at PO Box 91869, Austin, TX 78709, 512.891.6100.

Design and composition by Greenleaf Book Group and Kim Lance
Cover design by Greenleaf Book Group and Kim Lance

Cataloging-in-Publication data is available.

Print ISBN: 978-1-62634-363-4

eBook ISBN: 978-1-62634-364-1

Part of the Tree Neutral® program, which offsets the number of trees consumed in the production and printing of this book by taking proactive steps, such as planting trees in direct proportion to the number of trees used: www.treeneutral.com

Printed in the United States of America on acid-free paper

16 17 18 19 20 21   10 9 8 7 6 5 4 3 2 1

First Edition

"Is this the Complaint Department? Because I've got
A HUGE LIST of complaints, Mister!"

WORLD-CLASS CUSTOMER SERVICE

I KNOW YOU'RE BUSY, so I'll make this quick. We've all
suspected that America has become an impatient nation. Now
a poll from the Associated Press (AP) confirms this is, indeed,
fact. According to the poll, we've become a nation that gets
antsy after five minutes on hold, while on the phone, and after
15 minutes standing in a line. In another poll, almost one in four
people picked the grocery checkout line as the place where their

patience is most likely to melt, along with the ice cream in their cart. In short, we Americans want it all, and we want it NOW!

What greater proof do you need to realize that today's customers want the kind of service that exceeds their expectations? They want the kind of service that means they won't have to wait long for the results they want. Today's customers want **Fresh Customer Service.** Your commitment to reading this book and implementing my ideas about delivering Fresh Customer Service will lead to a **World-Class Customer Service Experience** that will, in turn, enhance your bottom line.

I can tell you, with complete confidence, that companies are still struggling to deliver an effective customer service experience—one that keeps customers satisfied, keeps them returning, and keeps them spreading the gospel of the company's services and products. Many of these same struggling companies have made a strong commitment to customer service, and that is critically important to the company's bottom line.

**"It's settled, then. Our new slogan is:
'Treat Every Customer Right.'"**

Yet, often times, the customer service commitment is delivered by an ill-defined, stale program. Short-term initiatives are force-fed to apprehensive employees utilizing such things as glossy print materials with vague, inadequate phrases: "Customers Are #1," "Treat Every Customer Right," and "Take Care of the Customer." These clichés often fall on deaf ears. Year after year, when they've racked their brains with catchy phrases, upselling, cross-selling—you name it—leaders and managers bang their heads against the wall in disbelief that customer service performance is still stagnant or, worse yet, declining.

The current trend in business is to downsize training and reduce funding to develop employees and instead spend those funds on making a great experience for the customer. In many businesses, reward and recognition (R&R) is seriously decreased, and the investment in employees is peanuts. Many of the customer service strategies being utilized today are outdated. Few actually work. Customers know the phrase, "You get what you pay for." Very often, they get much less than what they paid for—and they know it.

In this age, a customer can find your services duplicated, or your products for a cheaper price, on the next block. So, why use the same stale, outdated, failed approach to customer service?

The business world needs a makeover. A new perspective. A fresh approach. Fresh Customer Service demystifies how to attract loyal, happy customers who will return again and again. Not only that, they will recommend your business to their family and friends. This—what some may consider a minor detail—can actually tip the scales and be the difference between a prosperous organization and one that is bankrupt. So, what's the secret?

"I just don't think we're in the market for a customer service plan from 1943, Mr. Jenkins."

The Frontline Employee

The secret is actually more of an idea—one that began to blossom in me as a child growing up in Mississippi. It was rooted in my psyche at the start of my career, when I became a hardworking Frontline Employee. It is now the reason for my success. This idea is the key to unlocking sustained long-term success in whatever area of service or production is offered by your organization. Throughout your organization's entire process of selling, serving, marketing, cleaning—you name it—the only way you can hope to deliver a World-Class Customer Service Experience is by listening to, involving, and valuing the expertise and feedback provided by your Frontline Employees.

"No. It's not a prowler, it's an unpredictable market and pressure from shareholders that seems to rise by the hour."

What was that? What did I just hear? Were you just lamenting that customer service is only one more thing to worry about—a thorn in your side that is being twisted and pushed deeper by an unpredictable market and pressure from shareholders that seems to rise by the hour? I know, I know. The struggles to turn just-any-old-customer into a loyal customer is unyielding, and the burden of competition is so stiff you don't have time to think about what Mary Jo at the cash register, or Frank the janitor, has to say about things.

"Why does NO ONE take me seriously?"

Nevertheless, these are the exact people you need to listen to and to whom you should show your appreciation—the lady who answers customer complaint calls, the construction worker who is building a new home, the consultant who is trying to move a client, the nurse who cares for patients, the greeter who meets the customer at the entrance of the store, the cashier who tallies the customer's total at the register, the floor salesperson who explains why one appliance is better than the other, the bagger who offers to help carry grocery bags, the cleaner who tidies up the restrooms—the ones who always smile when they perform their duties.

"Heads I value my employees, tails I lay everyone off."

It includes anyone who comes in contact with the customer, whether it is face-to-face, via email, voice mail, snail mail, instant message, live chat, etc. If you are a manager, frontline leader, supervisor, entrepreneur, director, human resource representative, small business owner, or CEO, you can offer your Frontline Employees a healthy, fruitful, cohesive working environment, where their contribution is valued and respected. When you do this, the Frontline Employee will take care of your customers, the customers will be loyal to your organization, and it will be reflected in your bottom line.

"Good news. I'm raising the employees up
one notch in their value to me."

The employee is number one, not the customer. The customer is number two.

Since most customer service strategies are partially, or wholly, based on making the customer number one, then obviously customer service levels must be at an all-time high, right? Everywhere you go, people are raving about how great their daily customer service experiences are, and customer satisfaction polls back this affirmation with hard data.

I'll give you a moment to stop laughing before I continue. Hopefully, you didn't snort any of your morning coffee through your nose!

We all realize that, in far too many cases, the one word that best sums up the state of customer service today is "disaster." Yet, especially in an era where prices have already been slashed, customer service is more important than ever as a competitive differentiator.

The key to running a successful operation is believing in and practicing the concept that customers should always come second. Employees matter more in the immediate sense and should, therefore, come first. After all, happy employees unleash their enthusiasm and passion from within, and that passion is contagious. It infects everyone around them—including customers.

Frontline Employees need to feel appreciated, motivated, and important. If you ever hope to provide a World-Class Customer Service Experience through Fresh Customer Service, then you need to take care of the Frontline Employee first. Passionate and motivated employees deliver a World-Class Customer Service Experience quicker, better, and more consistently.

"Someday, as a frontline employee, all of this might possibly, kind of, sort of, if the stars align . . . be yours."

The Frontline Employee is the most important asset, resource, and ally to the operations of any organization. Every employee and his or her quest to deliver a World-Class Customer Service Experience is paramount. We must, first, take care of all our Frontline Employees if we ever hope to effectively and consistently reach the customer. We must treat each employee with the utmost trust, honesty, respect, integrity, and commitment to his or her well-being. We should always seek to maximize the talent of each employee and work to enhance his or her quality of life. We must also value diversity among our staff and work to fulfill their personal aspirations. Only then will the Frontline Employee be more apt to pour his or her heart into providing a World-Class Customer Service Experience to meet the goals and objectives of the organization.

Happy employees naturally provide superior customer service. So, thank your employees every day, let them be involved in the planning of the work affecting them, and treat them with the utmost respect and courtesy. Even in times when consumers are looking to do things quickly and cheaply, they will notice . . . and they will come back for more!

**"The warden put me on prison yard morale committee.
He says I'm a good ambassador for the organization."**

Empower Frontline Employees

In order to inspire pride, excitement, teamwork, and fulfillment in the workplace, all employees should have the ability to be involved in planning the work affecting them. In addition to providing a World-Class Customer Service Experience, you want to ensure that the Frontline Employee is an ambassador for the organization.

**"Ironing your own shirts — What is it you've done
wrong that you're trying to make right?"**

The company's objectives, goals, aspirations, and expected customer experience should be communicated to all employees. It is the responsibility of everyone to support empowerment of Frontline Employees. When the customer has a problem or a bad experience, the employee should have the permission, ability, and tools to **Make-It-Right Now** (this will be covered in depth in Fresh Step 3). The instant satisfaction of the customer is the responsibility of every employee. Help the Frontline Employee make the customer's problem his problem.

**"How could you forget the compass?!
Isn't that a navigational BASIC??!"**

Let Frontline Employees know the priorities

The priorities and values of the organization need to be crystal clear in the minds of all Frontline Employees. Forcing them to work in ambiguous uncertain "gray areas" of operation is like blindfolding the average person and asking them to walk a tightrope. It's simply a recipe for disaster. Whenever I take over a new team, I always establish a general theme or mission/priority statement. Here's one I have used before:

OUR TEAM
Always Exceeds Expectations!

Safely deliver a World-Class customer service experience that develops people, drives performance, and protects the company's assets.

**"It's a little unconventional, but the
crowds love the fresh approach."**

For many individuals, organizations, corporations, mom-and-pop stores, and entrepreneurs, delivering a World-Class Customer Service Experience through Fresh Customer Service will require a culture change. Embracing this experience, no matter how much work it takes, will deliver a competitive edge unlike any other. Our customers are asking—no, they are begging—for Fresh Customer Service. If we provide it, we will be able to deliver a World-Class Customer Service Experience *every* time. We can serve the customer and beat the competition. No company is successful, financially or otherwise, without Fresh Customer Service.

"Here at Fisher, Fisher & Fisher, we don't believe in 'OUT.'"

What are the concrete results of *Fresh Customer Service?*

While you're reading, keep in mind that, when Fresh Customer Service is implemented, you will see remarkable results.

"He's big on assessment but small on effective action."

- You'll be able to align corporate strategies to better incorporate the core mission of customer service and, ultimately, enhance the bottom line.

- You'll see an improved frontline execution of corporate strategies without sacrificing the customer experience.

- You'll be able to create awareness, empowerment, and tools that can be utilized by Frontline Employees to Make-It-Right Now—when customer problems or opportunities surface.

- You'll see an increased confidence in frontline staff for the resolution of customer issues and increased consistency in response.

- You'll have a competitive, grounded customer service program as a part of the core business model.

- Finally, you'll be able to boast a high-speed response to the market that will help in sustaining a competitive advantage, as opposed to responding in a reactive way that will place your organization in an inferior competitive position.

So, what, exactly, is Fresh Customer Service?

The definition of Fresh Customer Service consists of the following 6.5 steps:

- It's Fresh Understanding. . .
  - ⇨ Step 1. Side-By-Side Walking
  - ⇨ Step 2. Smart Tasking

- It's Fresh Empowerment. . .
  - ⇨ Step 3. Make-It-Right Power
  - ⇨ Step 4. What-If Arsenal

- It's Fresh Thinking. . .
  - ⇨ Step 5. Bubble-Up Innovation
  - ⇨ Step 6. Relentless Focus
  - ⇨ Step 6.5. Make It Happen Now!

**"Just so you know, I'd put the temperature of your
customer service at between RARE and MEDIUM RARE."**

This *Fresh Notes* book will take you on the journey of dis-
covering the 6.5 steps to the Fresh Customer Service Experience. You'll learn what Fresh Customer Service means, how to
spot it (or the lack thereof) in your everyday experiences, how
to implement it in your company, and how to instill it in your
work team. By the time you've read through these quick, easy,
fun Fresh Steps, you'll be ready to take the plunge and never go
back to yesterday's old, stale, incompetent service.

Study these 6.5 Fresh Steps, and your bottom line will increase.
Start putting these Fresh Steps into action, and your bottom line
will zoom upward. Really become serious about implementing
these 6.5 Fresh Steps with a relentless focus, and your bottom line
will move upward with the thrust of a space shuttle.

**"Your resumé is perfect, but do you know the
6.5 Steps of Fresh Customer Service?"**

6.5 STEPS OF FRESH CUSTOMER SERVICE

What does each of these 6.5 steps actually mean? First, I've compiled each of the steps for you and created a series of "pulse assessment" tests to help determine how far along you are in your efforts toward delivering Fresh Customer Service. I will also provide 6.5 Actions you can take to close any gaps you find in, and/or to enhance, your World-Class Customer Service Experience.

Ready to begin the 6.5 steps journey to delivering Fresh Customer Service that will lead to a World-Class Customer Service Experience to grow both your top and bottom line?

Great! Let's Go!

Let's start by completing the following self-assessment tests, noting the temperature of your current customer service and scoring points as shown in the following scale:

YOUR ANSWER	POINTS
Yes	2
No	0
Sort of	1

Fresh Step 1. Side-By-Side Walking

I'm pretty sure you've heard something similar to the phrase, "Before you judge a man, walk a mile in his shoes." To truly understand the perspective of another person, you must be able to experience the world as they see it. The first Fresh Step, **Side-By-Side Walking,** will teach you to how "walk a mile" in your employees' shoes, to view their work from their perspective, and to understand what they do and why they do it. This will, essentially, enable you to identify the gaps in your company's operations and help you determine which areas need improvement.

	QUESTIONS	YES/NO/ SORT OF	OUR SCORE
1.	Do you really understand what a usual day is like for your employee?		
2.	Do the policies of the company actually help to enhance the customer experience?		
3.	Will Side-By-Side walking with your employees for a day result in enhancing your image among your employees?		
		TOTAL SCORE:	

Fresh Step 2. Smart Tasking

Smart Tasking clearly defines the critical tasks and/or processes that support the customer offers and the deadlines by which they must be completed. The most important factor is completing the necessary tasks and/or processes without impeding the delivery of a World–Class Customer Service Experience to the customer. Smart Tasking creates harmony and balance between completing the tasks and/or processes and delivering a World–Class experience.

The second Fresh Step is important in setting up clear priorities and expectations for your employees to assist them in offering the best support to your customers. This helps in eliminating unnecessary work for the employees and makes their tasks more manageable and enjoyable.

	QUESTIONS	YES/NO/ SORT OF	YOUR SCORE
1.	Have you interacted with your customers to inquire about their experience and the service they've received?		
2.	Do you collect feedback on tasks and processes that have been put in place by your organization?		
3.	Is Smart Tasking important, according to you?		
		TOTAL SCORE:	

Fresh Step 3. Make-It-Right Power

Make-It-Right Power—Fresh Step 3—gives both responsibility and authority to the employees who are the most capable of satisfying a customer complaint or issue at any point in time. This empowers employees in resolving customer issues and complaints in order to enhance customer satisfaction.

	QUESTIONS	YES/NO/ SORT OF	YOUR SCORE
1.	Do you take regular feedback from your customers?		
2.	Do you take action to resolve customer complaints and issues?		
3.	Do you make improvements in your policies and processes to resolve the common problems encountered by your customers?		
	TOTAL SCORE:		

Fresh Step 4. The What-If Arsenal

The **What-If Arsenal** is a repository of tools, processes, techniques, and tips employees need in order to do their jobs in a manner that promotes the World-Class Experience. The What-If Arsenal builds on organizational experiences, reduces the need to design new solutions, and helps give Make-It-Right authority to Frontline Employees so they can instantly serve and satisfy the customer.

This is a set of tools and processes that is put in place to handle an upset customer. The What-If Arsenal is built on organizational experiences. It decreases the need to reinvent the wheel, while providing employees with a fresh pool from which to take fresh solutions to problems.

	QUESTIONS	YES/NO/ SORT OF	YOUR SCORE
1.	Do your customers receive the same level of response to their problems when the manager is away?		
2.	Pose a "what-if" situation to a new employee. Was that employee prepared to offer an instant solution?		
3.	Call one of your competitors with the same problem you asked your new employee. Are they better prepared in instantly solving the problem?		
	TOTAL SCORE:		

Fresh Step 5. Bubble-Up Innovation

Bubble-Up Innovation, the fifth Fresh Step, will show you how to appreciate and utilize the current ideas your Frontline Employees have for improving the entire organization. After all, Frontline Employees are the face of the company. They come in contact with customers every day—day-in and day-out. They, not managers or CEOs, are privy to why senior customers want earlier store hours, or why the trash that accumulates on the sidewalk is keeping customers away. It is a winning practice to listen to the comments and suggestions Frontline Employees may have to make your organization better. This step also helps in showing you ways to appreciate and utilize the ideas your employees offer.

	QUESTIONS	YES/NO/ SORT OF	YOUR SCORE
1.	Do your employees have the freedom to share their concerns, ideas, and feedback?		
2.	Does your organization encourage creativity and innovation?		
3.	Is there anything in your organization that will prevent the implementation of this step?		
		TOTAL SCORE:	

Fresh Step 6. Relentless Focus

Relentless Focus is the continual and consistent emphasis on the Frontline Employee delivering a World-Class Customer Service Experience and embedding this concept into your core business model, as opposed to implementing a customer service "program-of-the-month." Fresh Customer Service cannot be delegated to just one program per month, one part of the store, or even just the customer service department. Fresh Customer Service is an organization-wide initiative that extends from inside the store to the street corner and parking lot. It is an ongoing process. It must be embodied in each and every worker every minute of the day and in all areas of sales, production, marketing, management, ownership, and customer service.

This means consistent and continual emphasis on your employees to deliver World-Class Customer Service.

	QUESTIONS	YES/NO/ SORT OF	YOUR SCORE
1.	In your organization, is the focus on customer care steady and persistent throughout the year?		
2.	Is the emphasis on a high quality customer experience the same, no matter who is in charge?		
3.	Is everyone in your organization equally responsible for enhancing the customer experience?		
	TOTAL SCORE:		

Fresh Step 6.5. Make It Happen Now!

Finally, we've reached Fresh Step 6.5. That's right . . . you're not quite finished until you can **Make It Happen Now**! It's up to you to take it from here.

This is a step to remind you that all the other steps will do you no good unless and until you actually take action and make them happen.

	QUESTIONS	YES/NO/ SORT OF	YOUR SCORE
1.	Do you constantly review the tasks of your employees, ask for and take their input to update those tasks, as necessary?		
2.	Do your employees have all the resources and freedom of creativity to effectively and instantly resolve your customers' problems?		
3.	Are you actually taking the care of your employees seriously and making them your number One priority?		
	TOTAL SCORE:		

Total Temperature Check

Now it's time to sum up your score from all the tests to see if your organization is truly delivering Fresh Customer Service, or whether you're providing something less competitive. Please add up the total score for each section on the next page:

SUMMARY OF SCORES

Step 1: Side-By-Side Walking　　　　　　_____

Step 2: Smart Tasking　　　　　　　　_____

Step 3: Make-It-Right Power　　　　　　_____

Step 4: What-If Arsenal　　　　　　　　_____

Step 5: Bubble-Up Innovation　　　　　_____

Step 6: Relentless Focus　　　　　　　_____

Step 6.5: Make It Happen Now!　　　　_____

Grand Total　　　　　　　　　　　_____

When you have your total, locate the category under which your temperature falls:

0 – 8 Rare

Oh no! Your freshness thermometer is down. You need to carefully study all 6.5 steps in order to ramp up your game.

9 – 17 Medium Rare

Meh! You have put in a little effort, but it probably was ages ago. The bad news is that your customer service strategies and processes are going stale.

18 – 26 Medium

A cookie for you! The importance of Fresh Customer Service is understood by you and your organization; however, you may not be aware of the best ways to enhance your processes.

27 – 36 Medium Well

Bravo! You are almost there! You know the importance of Fresh Customer Service and are implementing those steps within your organization. Just a little more effort, and you will reach the top.

37 – 42 Well Done

Congratulations! Your customer service is as fresh as newly baked bread just out of the oven! You know the importance of putting your employees first, which has resulted in enhanced customer satisfaction. Keep up the good work!

TAKEAWAY

Based on your temperature score, the following are a few ideas you can use to implement the 6.5 Fresh Customer Service steps to help you enhance overall satisfaction.

6.5 Actions to take if your Temperature is Rare

Don't be discouraged if your total Fresh Customer Service temperature falls in the "Rare" range. There are lots of things you can do to freshen and enhance your customer service. Here are a few actions you'll want to implement right away:

1. Ensure that all tasks and process steps are being followed by your employees during the shift from the old way to the new.

2. Examine the various processes within your organization and determine exactly where the problems are and what improvements need to be made.

3. Recommend to your employees a specific time duration for each task.

4. All employees must be fully equipped with the **Make-It-Right** power to effectively encounter and resolve customers' problems and complaints.

5. Once you've gathered **What-If Arsenal** data, don't let it get buried. Ensure that your employees understand how to utilize that data in their daily interactions with customers.

6. Make the World-Class Customer Experience a major part of your corporate strategies, goals, and culture. Prevent it from turning into just another program of the month, which is usually forgotten as soon as the day is over.

6.5. Understand all 6.5 steps of Fresh Customer Service and start implementing them within your organization.

6.5 Actions to take if your Temperature is Medium Rare

All is not lost if your total Fresh Customer Service temperature is Medium Rare. The following 6.5 steps will help you to revamp your customer service strategies:

1. Thank all your employees frequently.

2. Spend time with your employees to learn and understand how they are resolving customer problems.

3. Remember that **Side-By-Side Walking** can only be beneficial to you if you are fully committed to the entire process. There are no shortcuts.

4. There should be **Relentless Focus** on embedding the practices and principles of Fresh Customer Service in your business culture.

5. Introduce **Smart Tasking** within your organization as it will help you in creating a harmonized balance between pro-cesses and/or task completion to deliver an outstanding customer service experience.

6. Make sure you are actively engaging all your employees in **Bubble-Up Innovation** activities.

6.5. Make all the 6.5 Fresh Customer Service steps happen in your organization.

6.5 Actions to take if your Temperature is Medium

You are going in the right direction if your total Fresh Customer Service temperature is Medium, but you may need a little guidance to keep going in the right direction. You can take the following 6.5 steps to enhance your customer service:

1. Ask your employees what would make it easier for them to resolve customer's problems.

2. Add a little fun element to Smart Tasking and ensure the daily tasks become more meaningful and easier for your employees.

3. Ensure there is a clear procedure and policy regarding the ways of administering **Make-It-Right** power. Keep it fun and simple.

4. Provide proper training to all your employees on the best ways of maintaining **Relentless Focus** while executing their tasks.

5. Introduce the **Bubble-Up Innovation** process within your company, as this will help you in appreciating and utilizing the ideas your customers provide for enhancing the overall organization.

6. Offer your employees the **What-If Arsenal** so they have the right tools when dealing with difficult scenarios, even when the manager is away.

6.5. Ensure that all 6.5 steps are efficiently executed. When your employees feel appreciated, empowered, and taken care of, they will properly take care of your customers.

6.5 Actions to take if your Temperature is Medium Well

You are doing a great job if your total Fresh Customer Service temperature is Medium Well! To continue on this path and to further enhance your customer service experience, take the following 6.5 steps:

1. Reflect and assess the tasks you did while doing **Side-By-Side Walking**. Note the problems that occurred, and compare them to the job descriptions of your employees.

2. Establish **Make-It-Right** authority for all employees in your organization.

3. Actively involve your employees in **Smart Tasking** by encouraging them to speak up whenever they believe they are performing tasks that are unnecessary, ineffective, or inefficient.

4. Ensure the **What-If Arsenal** is at your employee's finger-tips, or is safely stored in their heads, so they can instantly retrieve it when a complex scenario arises.

5. Keep encouraging innovation and creativity when it comes to resolving customer issues and complaints. Make sure your employees are comfortable in sharing their ideas.

6. Encourage **Relentless Focus** within your organization as it forces the company to make a continuing investment in offering a World-Class Customer Service Experience by implanting it in the core business model of the company.

6.5. Make all the 6.5 steps happen with commitment and effort.

6.5 Actions to take if your Temperature is Well Done

If your total Fresh Customer Service temperature is Well Done, then you have got it all figured out! Congratulations! At this point, you only have to maintain your freshness. To sustain and further enhance your customer service experience, you can take the following 6.5 steps:

1. Offer necessary training to your employees in order to main-tain your outstanding temperature.

2. Your employees must continue to be your number-one priority and your customers should be your second priority.

3. Make **Side-By-Side Walking** an annual or quarterly occurrence. This will help you in understanding the position of your organization and help you in determining what is working and what is not.

4. Make sure all employees are benefiting from **Make-It-Right** power. This power instills both authority and responsibility in resolving customer problems and complaints to your employees. This will help to maintain the freshness of your customer service.

5. Ensure that your employees have the freedom to brainstorm their own **What-If Arsenal** ideas in order to sustain your business by making your customer service experience grow.

6. Maintain **Relentless Focus** within your organization. It is a mind-set that must be continuously updated. Your employees must always have customer service in the front of their minds, whether they are top-level executives or entry-level personnel.

6.5. Keep on rocking with your Fresh Customer Service Experience!

ABOUT MICHAEL D. BROWN

MICHAEL D. BROWN is a sought-after speaker, global management expert, and author of *Fresh Passion: Get A Brand or Die A Generic, Fresh Customer Service®: Treat the Employee as #1 and the Customer as #2 and You Will Get Customers for Life, Fresh Passion Leadership: Become a Distinct, Branded Leader or An Extinct Generic, Fresh Notes on Personal Branding: Get A Brand or Die A Generic, Fresh Notes on Customer Service: Treat the Employee as #1 and the Customer as #2 and You Will Get Customers for Life,* and *Fresh Notes on How Not to Graduate into Poverty: Become a Distinct Brand or Extinct Generic.*

He has over eighteen years of experience helping companies and organizations—including US Army, US Marines, BP, Amoco, Capital One, Jason's Deli, Murphy Oil, Omni Hotels, Houston Rockets, Wells Fargo, Marriott, Ford Foundation, and Hampton University—achieve results and has held numerous leadership positions at Fortune Global 100 Companies.

Michael is a leading authority on delivering fresh results. His expertise in revamping how companies provide world-class customer service and establish a market-leading brand has led him to assisting individuals in creating personal brands that allow them to achieve otherwise unattainable levels of personal and professional success. He is recognized for this best-in-class coaching strategy that yields consistent results and for helping companies deliver double-digit growth to the top and bottom line. He holds an MBA in Global Management. Michael was ranked in the top 5% among high-performing sales leaders and coaches in leading Global Fortune 500 companies.

Michael has motivated and helped thousands of entrepreneurs, military personnel, individuals, college students, graduates, small business owners, and entrepreneurs move from a stage of generic mediocrity to an exciting place where they become successful personal brands that yield exponential personal economic and professional success. His signature work *Fresh Passion: Get a Brand or Die a Generic* is the catalyst for helping individuals make the transformation and achieving world-class success.

Michael's work has been featured in hundreds of publications and media outlets, including: *Forbes*, Georgia Public Radio, *Business Week*, NPR Radio, *The Economic Times*, *Business Education Forum*, *Bits and Pieces on Leadership*, *Inside Business*, *The Manager's Intelligence Report*, *Black Enterprise*, and *U.S. Business Review*.

RECEIVE MY FREE eNEWSLETTER AND 52 FRESH CUSTOMER SERVICE TIPS

I trust that you extracted value from this book. To continue receiving fresh and valuable information, please go to www.TheMichaelDBrown.com and sign up for the powerful eNewsletter and amazing 52 customer service tips.

ORDERING INFORMATION

Fresh Notes on Customer Service is available at Barnes & Noble, www.TheMichaelDBrown.com, Amazon, and other fine bookstores and online outlets. Please contact us for quantity discounts. The book is also available to the book trade and educators through all major wholesalers.

READY TO ENGAGE WITH A RESULTS-DRIVEN GLOBAL MANAGEMENT EXPERT, AUTHOR, SPEAKER, AND COACH?

To book Michael for speaking, coaching, training, and consulting engagements, please go to www.themichaeldbrown.com and submit a booking form.

BE SOCIAL WITH US

Join and follow us on